You Are My Sunshine

summersdale

YOU ARE MY SUNSHINE

Summersdale Publishers Ltd
46 West Street
Chichester
West Sussex
PO19 1RP
UK

www.summersdale.com

Printed and bound in the Czech Republic

ISBN: 978-1-84953-834-3

Substantial discounts on bulk quantities of Summersdale books are available to corporations, professional associations and other organisations. For details contact Nicky Douglas by telephone: +44 (0) 1243 756902, fax: +44 (0) 1243 786300 or email: nicky@summersdale.com.

To...

From...

Many people will walk
in and out of your life,
But only true friends
will leave footprints
in your heart.

Laszlo Kotro-Kosztandi

SHARED JOY

is a

DOUBLE JOY;

shared sorrow

is

half a sorrow.

Swedish proverb

You make the greyest of days brighter

The greatest healing
therapy is friendship
and love.

Hubert Humphrey

A friend is someone
who knows all about
you and still loves you.

Elbert Hubbard

Thank you for being you, and accepting me as I am

Friends are born, not made.

Henry Adams

Each friend represents
a world in us. A world
possibly not born
until they arrive.

Anaïs Nin

A GOOD FRIEND
is... a tie to
THE PAST,
a road to
THE FUTURE,
the key to
sanity.

Lois Wyse

A journey is best
measured in friends
rather than miles.

Tim Cahill

One doesn't know,
till one is a bit at odds
with the world, how
much one's friends who
believe in one rather
generously mean to one.

D. H. Lawrence

You lift me up when I'm down

I cherish everything about you

Against the assault
of laughter, nothing
can stand.

Mark Twain

A true friend... advises justly, assists readily, adventures boldly, takes all patiently, defends courageously, and continues a friend unchangeably.

William Penn

Ah, how good
it feels!
The hand of
an old friend.

Henry Wadsworth
Longfellow

Love is blind; friendship
closes its eyes.

Anonymous

A friend knows the song in my heart and SINGS IT TO ME when my memory fails.

Donna Roberts

You reassure me when I need it the most

Those who bring
sunshine into the lives
of others cannot keep
it from themselves.

J. M. Barrie

Not from the heavy soil
of the earth, but from the
spirit's choice and free
desire, needing no oath
of legal bond, is friend
bestowed on friend.

Dietrich Bonhoeffer

You push me to be the very best I can be

A day without **laughter** is a day wasted.

Nicolas Chamfort

I always felt that the great high privilege, relief and comfort of friendship, was that one had to explain nothing.

Katherine Mansfield

A FAITHFUL friend is the MEDICINE of life.

Ben Sira

A real friend is one who
walks in when the rest
of the world walks out.

Walter Winchell

I am wealthy in
my friends.

William Shakespeare

You know me better than I know myself

You believe in me even when I don't believe in myself

Good friends are like
stars; you don't always
see them but you
know they're there.

Anonymous

Friendship is unnecessary... It has no survival value; rather it is one of those things which give value to survival.

C. S. Lewis

When we give cheerfully and accept gratefully, everyone is blessed.

Maya Angelou

A friend is one of the
nicest things you can
have and one of the best
things you can be.

Douglas Pagels

I will
follow
you to the
ends of the
world.

Khaled Hosseini

You
constantly
push me
to better
myself

Friendship isn't
a big thing – it's a
million little things.

Anonymous

For love casts out
fear, and gratitude
can conquer pride.

Louisa May Alcott

Friends like you do not come along often

Some people go to priests; others to poetry; I to my friends.

Virginia Woolf

An unshared happiness
is not happiness.

Boris Pasternak

A friend *is someone* WHOSE FACE *you can see* IN THE dark.

Frances O'Roark Dowell

The friend who holds your hand and says the wrong thing is... dearer... than the one who stays away.

Barbara Kingsolver

Yes, we must ever be friends; and of all who offer you friendship Let me be ever the first, the truest, the nearest and dearest!

Henry Wadsworth Longfellow

Thank you
for all
that you've
taught me

You're
always
honest

For a friend with
an understanding
heart is worth no less
than a brother.

Homer

My thoughts are free
to go anywhere, but it's
surprising how often they
head in your direction.

Anonymous

No man is useless while he has a friend.

Robert Louis Stevenson

The finest friendships are
between those who can
do without each other.

Elbert Hubbard

Wherever you go, no matter what the weather, always BRING YOUR OWN sunshine.

Anthony J. D'Angelo

If you have nothing
in life but a good
friend, you are rich.

Michelle Kwan

There is no **investment** you can make which will pay you so well as the **effort** to scatter sunshine and good cheer.

Orison Swett Marden

People will forget what
you did, but people
will never forget how
you made them feel.

Maya Angelou

You
always
know how
to cheer
me up

Friendship needs no words - it is solitude delivered from the anguish of loneliness.

Dag Hammarskjöld

In the sweetness of
friendship let there
be laughter. For in the
dew of little things the
heart... is refreshed.

Kahlil Gibran

You
inspire me
every day

I have loved my
friends as I do virtue,
my soul, my God.

Thomas Browne

I keep my friends as misers do their treasure, because, of all things granted us by wisdom, none is greater or better than friendship.

Pietro Aretino

A GOOD
laugh is
sunshine
in the
house.

William Makepeace
Thackeray

You always
have
my best
interests
at heart

A friend is someone who gives you total freedom to be yourself – and especially to feel, or not feel.

Jim Morrison

Let us learn to show our friendship for a man when he is alive and not after he is dead.

F. Scott Fitzgerald

Never above you.
Never below you.
Always beside you.

Walter Winchell

I can trust my friends. These people force me to examine myself, encourage me to grow.

Cher

You're there even when we are miles apart

THE BEST mirror is an old friend.

Anonymous

But I have made him my
friend, and now he is
unique in all the world.

Antoine de Saint-Exupéry

Friends are those rare
people who ask how
we are and then wait
to hear the answer.

Ed Cunningham

You have
a heart
of gold

My friends
are my estate.

Emily Dickinson

The better part of
one's life consists of
his friendships.

Abraham Lincoln

You help
me to
see my
strengths

Their continued existence.

Christopher Hitchens, when asked 'What do you most value in your friends?'

To love, and to be
loved, is the greatest
happiness of existence.

Sydney Smith

WITH TRUE
friends
EVEN WATER
drunk
together is
SWEET ENOUGH.

Chinese proverb

You make
me laugh
even when I
don't want
to smile

The ornament of a
house is the friends
who frequent it.

Ralph Waldo Emerson

No love, no friendship,
can cross the path of our
destiny without leaving
some mark on it forever.

François Mauriac

One joy
scatters a
hundred
griefs.

Chinese proverb

You're the light at the end of the tunnel

Not a word passes
between us, not because
we have nothing to
say... because we don't
have to say anything.

Khaled Hosseini

Few delights can equal
the mere presence of one
whom we trust utterly.

George MacDonald

A friend is a gift you give yourself.

Robert Louis Stevenson

I know
that I can
always
turn to you

God, or what I would
call the power of
creation, seems to favour
human beings who
accept and love life.

Arthur Rubinstein

I can no other answer make, but thanks, and thanks, and ever thanks.

William Shakespeare

Sometimes people are
beautiful. Not in looks.
Not in what they say.
Just in what they are.

Markus Zusak

Fate chooses our relatives,
we choose our friends.

Jacques Delille

You give
the best
advice

There is nothing **I would not do** for those who are *really my friends.* I have no notion of **loving people** BY HALVES.

Jane Austen

Count your age by friends,
not years. Count your
life by smiles, not tears.

Anonymous

A true friend is
forever a friend.

George MacDonald

You know how to make me laugh with just a look

A REAL
friendship
should not fade
AS TIME PASSES,
and should not
weaken
because of
SPACE SEPARATION.

John Newton

Laughter is a sunbeam of the soul.

Thomas Mann

I can't be
angry when
you're
around

If I had a flower for every
time I thought of you...
I could walk through
my garden forever.

Anonymous

I would rather walk with
a friend in the dark,
than alone in the light.

Helen Keller

A GOOD companion shortens THE longest road.

Turkish proverb

You listen when I have a problem

The best way to cheer
yourself is to try to cheer
somebody else up.

Mark Twain

Rare as is true love, true friendship is rarer.

Jean de La Fontaine

There's nothing worth
the wear of winning,
But laughter and the
love of friends.

Hilaire Belloc

Words are easy,
like the wind;
Faithful friends are
hard to find.

Richard Barnfield

You take
away sadness
and replace
it with
happiness

A FRIEND ☀

is the one who

will overlook your

BROKEN FENCE,

and instead admire the

flowers 🌼

in your garden.

Anonymous

I got you to look after me,
and you got me to look
after you, and that's why.

John Steinbeck

A good friend is so much
cheaper than therapy.

Anonymous

You make life better by just being a part of it

Some friendships are
made by nature, some by
contract, some by interest,
and some by souls.

Jeremy Taylor

The greatest gift of life is **friendship,** and I have received it.

Hubert Humphrey

You always encourage me to keep trying

Our triumphs seem hollow
unless we have friends
to share them, and our
failures are made bearable
by their understanding.

James Rachels

A friend is a person
with whom I may be
sincere. Before him,
I may think aloud.

Ralph Waldo Emerson

I feel that there is **nothing** more truly **artistic** than to **love people.**

Vincent Van Gogh

You
always
lift my
spirits

A friend is one soul
abiding in two bodies.

Aristotle

True happiness is... the friendship and conversation of a few select companions.

Joseph Addison

I love you not because
of who you are but
because of who I am
when I am with you.

Roy Croft

Friendship is always a
sweet responsibility,
never an opportunity.

Kahlil Gibran

You never fail to brighten my day

I love
HUGGING.
I wish I was an
octopus,
so I could hug
ten people
AT A TIME.

Drew Barrymore

Friends are the
bacon bits in the
salad bowl of life.

Anonymous

I felt it shelter to
speak to you.

Emily Dickinson

A day
spent with
you is a
day well
spent

You can't deny laughter;
when it comes, it plops
down in your favourite
chair and stays as
long as it wants.

Stephen King

A friend is worth all hazards we can run.

Edward Young

You
always
know the
right thing
to say

There is no exercise
better for the heart
than reaching down
and lifting people up.

John Andrew Holmes

If you want others to be happy, practice compassion. If you want to be happy, practice compassion.

Dalai Lama

There is nothing
BETTER
than a friend.
unless it is
A FRIEND
with
chocolate.

Linda Grayson

You take
pride in my
accomplishments

Friendship is the only cement that will ever hold the world together.

Woodrow Wilson

For you, a **thousand** times over.

Khaled Hosseini

Without friends no one would choose to live, though he had all other goods.

Aristotle

Friendship is born at that moment when one says to another: 'What! You, too? I thought I was the only one.'

C. S. Lewis

Nothing changes when we've been apart

The jewel in my dower,
I would not wish
Any companion in
the world but you.

William Shakespeare

For friendship makes
prosperity more shining
and lessens adversity by
dividing and sharing it.

Cicero

Best friend,
my well-spring
in the wilderness!

George Eliot

Your zest
for life is
contagious

There is one friend
in the life of each of us,
who seems not a separate
person, however dear and
beloved, but an expansion,
an interpretation,
of one's self.

Edith Wharton

Only your real friends will tell you when your face is dirty.

Sicilian proverb

You remind me that whilst there is rain, there are also rainbows

A man's friendships
are one of the best
measures of his worth.

Charles Darwin

Friendship, like phosphorus, shines brightest when all around is dark.

Anonymous

FRIENDSHIP *is a* SHELTERING tree.

Samuel Taylor Coleridge

I value your honesty and integrity

The best friend is the man who in wishing me well wishes it for my sake.

Aristotle

The road to a
friend's house is
never long.

Danish proverb

Since there is nothing
so well worth having
as friends, never lose a
chance to make them.

Francesco Guicciardini

A single real friend is a
treasure worth more than
gold or precious stones.

G. D. Prentice

You're like a shooting star in a clear night's sky

Friendship is the greatest
of worldly goods.
Certainly to me it is the
chief happiness of life.

C. S. Lewis

You're
a ray of
sunshine

For more information about our books, find us on Facebook at **Summersdale Publishers** and follow us on Twitter at **@Summersdale**.

www.summersdale.com